The Event-Filled Life

Linda S. Beck

ISBN: 978-0-578-03457-7

The Forward

As soon as my first book, My Sanctuary, was published, people began encouraging me to *write* another book. I told everyone that over the last sixteen years, I have written enough stories to publish at least three more books. It was ironic that within a week, God gave me ten *new* stories.

The question in my mind was how to determine which stories would best go together. I sorted through all the ones that were left on the computer. Some of the early stories were typed before I got a computer. I found it interesting that over twenty of the titles on the computer started with *THE*. On occasion, the titles were changed when published in the newspaper; but as I reviewed them, I realized that all these stories are about eventful things that happened in my life. As each event took place, it taught me some valuable lessons about which events are really important in life, and which ones are "pieces of fluff." (I almost used that as the title of the book, but some of these events were more important lessons that God taught me about my personal response and use of the word…*THE*.)

It is significant how very important some little two and three-letter words *ARE* in *OUR* lives; *THE* first *AND* foremost being *GOD*. He *WAS* with me during these events and if *YOU* allow *HIM* to be in your life, He *MAY* teach *YOU* some lessons, *TOO*.

> In Revelations 3:20, Jesus said: "Here I am! I stand at the door and knock. If anyone hears my voice and opens the door, I will come in and eat with him, and he with me."

The Table of Contents

THE BEACH

Well, I made it to the beach and back, and I'm so glad I didn't back out on traveling. My family invited me to go, and I had been looking forward to it. I had not been to the beach since 2001 because of my health problems, and I wasn't sure how my body would react to four hours on the road.

I first wanted to try driving so I could take my cart along and maintain some independence, but Hurricane Ivan convinced me not to do that. I hate driving in the rain, and especially after dark, so I agreed to allow the family to push me around in a standard wheelchair.

I don't think they were fully aware of what a burden I would be. The unit we stayed in was very nice, but it wasn't handicapped accessible, and that created some difficult situations for all of us. Most of these we found solutions for, but I nearly fell several times.

After a couple months of therapy, my shoulders and arms were feeling better and I had just started using a walker again. After just a few attempts with the walker, the pain was worse.

Fortunately, it was time for therapy on Tuesday after we returned on Sunday. That has given me some pain relief. The doctor gave me samples of some stronger pain medication, and encouraged me to use it though I am reluctant to take anything stronger.

Thursday night and Friday, the wind blew at least 30-40 miles per hour, but it was a warm wind. Saturday was a beautiful sunny day, and the wind was calmer. It was in the low 80's, and the kids had a delightful time. Even baby Hallie liked the sand and water. A few times she put sand in her mouth, but it didn't seem to bother her. It was nice having more time to play with six-month-old Hallie. She is such a good baby. I love my grandchildren so much; they can be very entertaining.

As much as I love watching the ocean, I really don't much care to get in the sand anymore. Since I was only able to take sponge baths, I didn't want to get too dirty.

We went to several restaurants, and ate in the condo part of the time. I finally got to visit a Barnes and Noble Bookstore, and I really enjoyed that. Other than these events, I mostly sat on the balcony, and read some good books.

The beach is such a relaxing place, and I always dread leaving. I've never stayed long enough to get tired of being there. I must say, however, when we drove into my driveway, I was delighted to be home. It was really special because my niece's husband, Chris, had been there and mowed my yard. Everything looked so beautiful; it is always good to get home. I am particularly thankful for my handicapped accessible doll house.

THE BEGINNING

In everything there is a beginning. Have you ever given much thought to all the beginnings included in your life? Here are some examples:

...a time to be born

...a time to be an infant; a toddler

...a time of pre-school; kindergarten

...elementary school, middle school, high school

...college (or trade school)

...the school of hard knocks

Each of these is a new beginning and is an important time in our lives. Some of these early memories are through pictures, home movies, videos, DVD's (or whatever the new-fangled things will be called in the future.)

All childhood memories are not necessarily good ones. That depends on how well a child was treated, both physically and verbally. As an older wiser adult, I now realize that children should be punished in private, not ridiculed in public. These are often some emotionally damaging times that teach us valuable lessons. Sometimes children say or do cruel things to each other. I know a little girl that has just finished kindergarten and is getting ready for a new season. She is a beautiful child with sparkly eyes and dimpled cheeks. Some children have called her fat and made her feel bad about herself. One of the most painful things is to be given a *label:* fatty, skinny, ugly, nerd, and there are many more to choose.

Another troublesome time is those teenage years. During that time, peer pressure begins to change attitudes, habits, and quite frequently, even appearances. Teenagers face so many challenges as they make new friends (or sometimes enemies) during those trying years. A mother begins to wonder what happened to that boy or girl to whom she gave birth. (I'm not sure what fathers think, but I know life can become difficult for everyone involved.)

Then along comes love. There's a series of movies with perfect names to describe these times in some of our lives: "Love Comes Softly," "Love's Abiding Joy," etc. There used to be a saying something like this: "Love and marriage go together like a horse and carriage." So often this love leads to marriage and a baby carriage, and a new life cycle begins again.

Just like there is always a beginning, everything also has an end. Christians, however, have the promise of eternal life in heaven with our Heavenly Father. Knowing this, the end of our lives is not so scary. Are you ready to face the end of life peacefully? If not, get a copy of a Bible, pray and seek the help of a Christian friend or minister that can help you find that peace.

THE BELL SHEEP

Elvis Aaron Presley was born on January 8, 1935. Most everyone knows some of the history of his life, and many of us were (and still are) true Elvis fans. I thought he was the best looking man I've ever seen, and even now I love to hear him sing gospel music.

In the beginning of his career, many parents didn't want their kids to watch or listen to him because of his gyrating moves and sexy ways. (Lord, help, look at what is on television today.) As his stardom rose, even older people became his fans.

During the month of January and again during August, in remembrance of his death (August 16, 1977), there are several programs on public television about him. I have heard these recordings many times over the years and there have been several interesting things told about the *Christian* Elvis. There are those who judge him as having been addicted to drugs and alcohol. He was condemned for the number of women in his life, his failed marriages, and other vices.

Elvis was raised as an only child by a Christian mother and as many little boys do, he idolized his mama. I have always believed that he never really got over her death and had she lived through more of his career, perhaps his life would have been different.

Elvis had a love for gospel music and I believe he had a "personal relationship with the Lord." Some of the people who knew him intimately told interesting things that happened, as follows:

Many of his fans called Elvis "the King," which he didn't really like. Once in a concert, a long row of women stood up with a huge banner proclaiming him "King."

It was told that he stopped the music and said, "Jesus Christ is our King" or something close to that. (I didn't know I was going to feel that I should write this story; I wish I had taken some notes.)

At another concert, he was getting sick with the flu and didn't come out at the opening as he normally would have. Someone went and found him backstage on his knees asking God to give him strength to present a pleasing concert because "these people paid a lot of money tonight and came a long way to hear me."

When Elvis first announced that he wanted to make a gospel album, the record producers and others tried to stop him from doing so, but he loved to "worship the Lord through song" and his gospel music is still bought and loved by so many folks.

There was a televangelist, Rev. Rex Humbard that Elvis loved to watch. When he came on, Elvis would stop everything else to hear him preach. When Rev. Humbard and his wife visited Elvis in Los Vegas at a concert, he was invited backstage and they prayed together on their knees.

Humbard told a story on PBS about how he talked to Elvis about being a "bell sheep." He explained how a lead sheep in a flock has a bell around its neck which causes the other sheep to follow him. He told Elvis that because of all the fans who worshiped him that he believed Elvis could win fans over to worship the true King, our Lord and Savior Jesus Christ. Did Elvis lead people to Christ? We will never know, but God is a forgiving, loving God and knows the plans He has for us.

Rev. Humbard was asked by Elvis' father to speak at the funeral in August 1977. Elvis was a sinner just like the rest of us, but I think his death probably led a lot of people to the Lord, and his music possibly continues to do so. When I hear him sing, "How Great thou Art," I know who he is praising. Do you?

THE *BIGNESS* OF MY GOD

I wrote a story about how God can make our "rough places smooth." (Isaiah 42:16) Then I heard Joel Osteen speak about how God can make "small things big." As I listened, I realized he was talking about the "big" things God is doing in my life; I felt another story coming along.

My early memory goes back to being a skinny, shy little girl in a small mill village in Yadkin, NC. In my adult years, because of "big" health problems and medication, my body became a lot "bigger," but there was a dark period of time when I didn't know how "big" my God is. He continued to become bigger in my life, and with health changes, diet and exercise, I became "smaller." (Not so skinny, but smaller; lost 24 pounds again, ladies!)

When I started writing for publication, my short stories, or messages, began to grow in meaning, if not in length. A small audience of readers began to grow, and people began to stop me in restaurants, shops, and on the street to express their appreciation for how my stories touch them. Phone calls and emails came encouraging me to put the stories in a book. My Sanctuary was born, and with the help of my older daughter and the blessing of my "BIG GOD," the book was published.

My daughter researched and found Lulu.com on the internet. It is a print-on-demand publisher and I was told the book could "go out all over the world." In my "small" mind, I only saw the surrounding counties.

Imagine my surprise when my answering machine showed I had received a call from Washington, DC. This was the first of several "big events" since the first book was published. The message went like this:

> "Linda, this is Elizabeth Dole, Liddy, to my Salisbury friends, and I'm sorry to miss you today, but I look forward to talking to you soon. My husband is in the hospital and is coming along fine. I've been reading your book, My Sanctuary, and it is just marvelous. You are indeed a gifted writer. Just know I have great admiration for you, and for all you are accomplishing. God bless you and thank you so much for sharing your life to help so many people. I will look forward to talking to you soon. Bye now."

Later she called back and we talked. I have always admired her in a "big" way, just as I have Joni Eareckson Tada. Both ladies have done so much for others, and I pray I can follow their examples.

In my "small" mind, my book is not equal to the talents given to these ladies, but my "big" God seems to have plans for my "little" stories. Two days later, I learned that Ingram Distributors has purchased some copies of my book from Lulu.com, so the book really is being sold throughout the country at least, and maybe the world.

I started with one hundred copies and have since ordered fifty more. The bookstores are now ordering from their distributor and only my "awesome God" knows the plans he has for me and my books. (Jeremiah 29:11-13)

In his service, Joel Osteen said: "If you are not faithful where you are, you will never get where you want to be." He also said, "Small beginnings build the foundation for large things."

I think my early stories were the foundation that has become stronger through my Bible studies and reading and listening to Christian speakers. Osteen said that our growth begins in our roots. Then there is a period of fertilizing, hoeing, and watering before we reach the harvest. Is My Sanctuary my first season of harvest? Will God send this book throughout the world? First Corinthians 3:7 reads: "So neither he who plants nor he who waters is anything, but only God, who makes things grow."

Job 8:7 reads: "Your beginnings will seem humble, so prosperous will your future be." Osteen added, "Your latter days will be better than your former days when you are faithful. Sometimes we have to pass the tests of "smallness to reach greatness." No matter how long it takes, I must keep reminding myself that my due season is ahead.

My greatest desire is that my stories will be an inspiration to others that God will use the book so my "planting" can glorify Him.

THE BUGS IN MY LIFE

I wrote stories about the fires in my life, the pets, the coat, and the tray, so I decided to write this one about some of the bugs in my life. I do not like bugs inside, especially flies or roaches. A friend of mine likes bugs and she said she never kills them; not even in her house. She says they are God's creatures. Well, maybe when I kill them, they will go to "bug heaven."

I had my new home inspected and sprayed; the only problem I'm having inside is flies. I guess the wet cool spring caused them to want to come in out of the rain. They lined up in formation around the doorframe waiting for their chance. I think they discovered it takes a person in a wheelchair more time to get the door closed. Someone said I should spray around the doorframe and that might discourage the flies.

I believe these are "Japanese flies" because they come at me like kamikaze pilots.

They dive bomb around my head when I'm in bed or sitting in my recliner. Several have landed in my hair and tried to get in my ears when I am dozing. Of course, the fly swatter is often out of my reach. My house is not dirty and I don't have garbage around, but I have flies anyway. I warn them a few times, but then I transfer to my wheelchair and go in search of my weapon. I'm sorry, but I know where their feet have been in the pasture, and I don't want them near my food or my body. (I'm thankful there are not as many as there were in The Plague of Flies in Exodus 20:32.)

Is a bee a bug? Are bees considered insects? I don't know much about science, but I do have an interesting bee story. A carpenter bee is a bee that does not live in colonies, and bores tunnels into wood to lay their eggs. At my husband's home place, there were a large number of these that riddled holes into an outside storage shed. I always had to dodge these as I entered the building. My husband said they would not sting and since I never got stung, I could only assume he was correct.

My new house has vinyl siding so I thought there was no where for carpenter bees to drill holes. Once I wrote a story about buying a plastic clothes dryer rack, and how pleased I was that it would no longer mildew like the cheap wooden ones did. I realize now that the stand is still wooden, only the racks are plastic.

I kept seeing a bee buzzing around on my back porch and realized finally that it was like those from so many years ago. Then one day, I began to notice sawdust on my porch. I would sweep it off and the next day, it would be there again. Several extra holes appeared in the wooden dowels that hold the rack together. Finally, one day I watched the culprit work her way into one of the small holes. I thought about stopping up the hole with chewing gum, but as long as that bee stays outside, I'll just let her drill tunnels into my rack. It should be a few years before the bee totally destroys the rack, unless she begins to bring some friends or family with her.

The worse bugs I ever had were back when I was a new bride in Indianapolis, Indiana. I was hungry for some ole' Southern grits, so I went to a very large grocery store. I searched and finally asked for help. The stockman said, "Well, we used to have some." He took me to another section with what appeared to be a small empty cubbyhole. Way in back he found one small bag of grits. He said they had been there a long time.

I was elated! I couldn't wait to cook them. When I opened the bag at home, it was full of bugs! I had never encountered anything like that before and I was so disappointed. I had to come back to the South to get my grits.

When I used to work out in my yard, I generally just moved bugs out of my way. After all, I was on their turf then. A few times I sat down on some ant colonies and then, I was the one who moved. There were other bugs in my life, but I'm thankful I never lived in filthy conditions like some poor people have to do. Some of the documentaries on TV show bugs crawling all over babies, and it just breaks my heart to realize people live like that. Even when I lived in the apartment, it was sprayed about every three months, and I rarely saw a bug until just a few days before scheduled spray time.

This story has no real purpose other than putting my thoughts on paper. When one lives alone and has no one to talk to, sometimes it is a release to share one's thoughts in the form of a story, just for the heck of it!

THE BUZZARDS ARE CIRCLING

The Buzzards are Circling, but God's Not Finished with Me Yet is the name of a book that an elderly gentleman sent me in 2002 after reading about my major multiple sclerosis attack.

I couldn't help thinking about this title when I turned my cart over again out in my yard. Nothing was broken, but I was lying in the grass with the blazing sun bearing down on me. Looking up, I saw several buzzards circling overhead.

Fortunately, I had my phone and called my neighbor, Debbie, to see if she could get another neighbor's attention. My whole family had just left on vacation that morning and I can't remember phone numbers unless they are programmed into my phone.

As I became hotter, I told Debbie I had no choice but to call 911. At that point only my pride was hurt, but I know heat doesn't agree with some multiple sclerosis victims. One should never play around, even though I was trying to see the humor in another bad situation.

I told the 911 operator that I was not hurt and asked him to please have assistance come without blaring sirens. He said the fire truck had to come, but he would ask them to come quietly. In less then twenty minutes, three guys from the Woodleaf Fire Department had me up and in the shade.

Debbie stayed on the phone with me while I waited for the *cavalry* to come. She thought I was joking when I told her the buzzards were circling. She couldn't see them from her house. She was overly worried about me, so I had to joke with her a bit. I told her that buzzards like eyeballs and dead flesh. For some reason, she didn't think anything was very funny, until I was safely inside.

If I had not had my phone with me, it could have been very dangerous. If we didn't have volunteers that can step away from their work and come to help folks like me…well, it sure beat trying to crawl through the grass. As I waited for help, I did slide enough to get my face in the little bit of shade that the cart provided.

Some friends are wondering what I was doing out at the back of my property. Well, the mowers had come for the first time that spring and my yard looked so pretty. Two years before, I had some brush cut along the property line, and it had been chopped into two piles of mulch. I decided to take my gallon pail and spread mulch around the trees. After I fell, I waited until later in the day to do the front yard, and until the next day to do the new plants in the back yard. Believe me I turned the speed down to a snail's pace when I scooted along working from my scooter after this episode.

I've loved doing yard work since my husband and I purchased our first property when I was only nineteen. We had really become active in flowers and landscaping before my husband died. We had so many beautiful flowers and trees, and now the desire of my heart is to do my yard in a similar way, but on a smaller scale. I have to pay to have some of the work done, but I enjoy doing as much as I can from my scooter or wheelchair. Those buzzards might come a little closer next time, but I guess God wasn't through with me yet.

> "I called on the Lord in my distress. I cried to my God for help. He heard my voice from his temple, and my cry for help reached his ears." (Psalm 18:6)

THE CHANCES I TAKE

Do you believe in taking chances? Some people tell me I take too many risks. Maybe I do, but Second Timothy 1:7 reads: "For God did not give us a spirit of timidity, but a spirit of power, of love, and of self-discipline."(NIV) or "For God hath not given us the spirit of fear; but of power, and of love, and of a sound mind." (KJV)

People today find it hard to believe I was once a very shy little girl that never knew what to say or do. But I was, and I remember some things that contributed to that. When I was a child, some adults in my life often said or did things that shamed me in front of my peers. Somewhere a long the way, I drew back like a turtle's head retreats into the shell. My Father God took fear and shame out of my heart and mind when He called me to travel and speak in the name of the Lord Jesus Christ.

Recently, someone told me that humans are like animals; when animals are injured, they retreat and lick their wounds. I've never thought of it in those terms, but if I close my eyes and allow myself to visualize, I can picture where I did that a few times myself. Unfortunately, animals often make the same mistake twice. Just because they almost got hit while crossing the road once, does not mean they will not cross the road again, if and when, there is something on the other side that gets their attention. After they are injured once, and maybe twice, they no longer have the opportunity to "lick their wounds."

I suppose it may be the same with taking chances. Sometimes accidents happen even when we have done the same thing a dozen times over. That is probably the reason I haven't been using the walker much lately. Several times I tried walking and then fell; so I've been reluctant to risk falling again. With osteoporosis, I'm almost guaranteed to break something. (And it may end up being my "spirit," in addition to a bone. I've spent way too much time in the hospital during the summer in the past.)

But these are not the chances or risks I first started writing about. From the viewpoint of some, my greatest risks are in riding my scooter such long distances all over town. This particular day I decided to ride from Fifth Street to Whitehead Avenue in Spencer past North Rowan High School. A friend asked what I would have done if the scooter had stopped like it did the week before. Well, if so, I would have called 911 just as I did when I got stuck in front of the castle on Fulton Street.

My older daughter fears that someone will attack me. Well, they would be disappointed because I don't carry much of any value. I told her if anything happens, she should find peace with the fact that I died doing what I wanted to do.

When my husband first planned to buy a motorcycle at age nineteen, his mother wanted me to stop him from doing so. My seventeen-year-old mind replied, "I can't do that and if anything happens, I will find peace that he died doing what he wanted to do."

I guess in some ways, my scooter is possibly as dangerous as a motorcycle, or worse, because it is slower and smaller. But telling me not to ride the scooter is like telling a pedestrian not to walk on the sidewalk, or the joggers not to run, or the bicyclists not to pedal.

I appreciate that folks are concerned, but I get rather tired of being told by others what I "can" and "can't" do. For everything "I can't do," I find something "I can do." I've had a hassle with the State of North Carolina Driver's License Division off and on since 1989. At that time, it was just because I answered "yes" to a question about seizures. I've learned more every day that "ignorance of the law is no excuse." Also, some of these employees whose salaries we help pay through our tax money are often rude, and seem to enjoy reminding me that a driver's license is a "privilege, not a right."

I always try to follow rules, and I never drink and drive. I'd prefer not to drive illegally; that's a chance I would rather not take. But I've always been the one to decide not to drive if and when I doubted my safety; I'm ready to take a chance driving again now because I know I can. The employees of the Driver's License Division have no way of knowing whether I am really able or not.

My doctor said in 1996 when I started driving again, that he had no problem because anyone can have a seizure on the spur of the moment. I've been on medication since 1989, and thanks be to God, I have not had another seizure.

And then there is the issue of the damage to my legs in the 2002 multiple sclerosis exacerbation. I did have hand controls installed on my car in 2004. Once again, I've come a long way since then, and I don't know anyone who drives with their left leg. If I did not think I would be safe without hand controls, I wouldn't seek to have those restrictions removed.

Every time you or I get on the highways or byways today, we are taking chances. No matter how safe we try to be, or how good we can drive, some unlicensed person, who isn't even a US citizen, takes a "chance" that he or she will not be stopped by the police. Then there is the drunken driver who takes a "chance" that he, or she, may or may not, have a wreck and kill someone. And that innocent victim took a "chance" that day also.

Yes, I'm game to taking chances, but there's one belief I do not take chances with. And those who do not know or recognize Jesus Christ as their Lord and Savior are taking a chance on where they will spend eternity. Now that is one issue I have resolved, and no multiple sclerosis attack, vehicle wreck, or any other chance I take will change my plan to live eternal life in heaven. Are you taking any chances with your salvation as you walk, jog, or drive on these highways? I pray that you will resolve that issue, and please don't worry about me.

THE COAT

When I was a little girl, I mostly wore hand-me-downs or homemade clothes. Grandma made skirts for me from feed sacks and when they became too short, she would add a contrasting strip around the bottom.

Grandma made them by hand and now I appreciate how hard she worked making those skirts. She loved me very much and sacrificed for me. I remember when she purchased a red, white, and navy striped sweater for me from the Sears Roebuck Catalog. It cost about $6.00 and was my most treasured garment until my arms were longer than the sleeves. I am sure that was a lot of money for her at that time, but she was trying to thank me for things I had done for her when she fell and broke her arm. Thanks were not necessary, but I remember how special she made me feel.

I know there were many children who had even less of a wardrobe, but I remember how I envied those who had more. When I was a teenager and had my first real job, other than cleaning houses and ironing, I purchased two special outfits for my senior year in high school. I was especially proud because I had worked all summer to save the money. Those outfits were the closest I had come to owning the current styles, although they were actually cheap imitations of the brand-name items.

As time passed, other kinds of things became more important than clothes. Like so many other people, I worked to accumulate things of necessity, as well as frivolous things. When ill health and the death of my husband in 1993 changed my life, "things" suddenly meant nothing to me. I either sold or gave away almost everything I owned.

After several years of grieving, then healing and losing weight, I finally had to go shopping for a new wardrobe. As time passed, I developed a passion for pretty clothes and indulged myself in buying some special garments.

Enter THE COAT! The minute I put it on, I knew it was THE COAT!

It was more expensive than I usually would consider buying, but after all, it was ON SALE! My oldest daughter was shopping with me and said, "Mama that is THE COAT for you. You deserve it! Don't think about the price. Buy THE COAT!" With a coach like that, how could I resist?

Everywhere I wore THE COAT, people admired it. I was even told I looked *elegant* in it. Me – elegant! Wow!

I had never even looked elegant in my borrowed prom dress or used wedding dress. I was so proud I must have puffed up like a peacock when his feathers are fully spread. I had never had any garment so admired by others, and I guess I became a little cocky about THE COAT!

When a waitress accidentally dripped two drops of coffee on that lovely winter white wool, I was crushed. It happened on a Sunday morning when I was on my way to church, and I had to remind myself to be Christ-like. I prayed that God would help me get rid of the anger. ("A person's wisdom gives him patience; it is to his glory to overlook an offense." (Psalm 19:11) Fortunately, the cleaners removed most of the spot and I continued to enjoy wearing THE COAT that first season.

In the spring, I decided not to take any chances that moths might destroy my coat. I took the coat and a wool blazer to the cleaners to be properly cleaned and stored. I asked if I needed a receipt and was told they did not give receipts.

"Just call a week ahead when you want to get it out of storage," the clerk said. (I thought about how Judge Wapner on "The People's Court" said that one should *always* get a receipt.) But because I have a friend that leaves clothes stored there every year, I left THE COAT.

Okay, get out your crying towel. Now you can feel sorry for me! I went to pick up my coat and you guessed it...THE COAT was missing. I felt physically sick and emotionally distraught because I was sure I would never be able to replace THE COAT. Does it really matter in the scheme of things? Should I allow any material thing to mean that much to me?

The cleaners agreed to negotiate on the purchase of another coat. The store found they could order a coat like it from the manufacturer. Am I happy now? Is this the end of the story? I'm not sure, but with all the worry and frustration, I think the joy of ownership has been tarnished. Maybe I was too proud! Will I still wear THE COAT so proudly?

The moral of the story: "Pride goes before destruction, a haughty spirit before a fall." Proverbs 16:18 (NIV)

(UPDATE 2009: THE COAT is still beautiful, but I keep it at home now. So far there has been no damage due to moths. Because of my health problems, it hangs in my closet now more than I am able to wear it; but I still love THE COAT!)

THE COINCIDENCES OF PUBLISHING A BOOK

More and more things keep happening as a result of the publication of my first book, My Sanctuary. My card-ministry partner, Debbie, told me to take notes because they would become a story, and she was absolutely right. So here goes…

I've said it before…in the life of a Christian, there are no coincidences. In my personal dictionary, coincidence means "God at Work." Since the publication of my book, God has been real busy in my life.

A lady I know has multiple sclerosis and we talk from time to time. One day she called about my cards. After some discussion, I asked if she had heard about my new book. She had not, but immediately asked if she could get one. I asked a friend to take me to Spencer for lunch with Ann. The next morning after having read the whole book, she called and said: "You need to write another book."

I told her I didn't need to write another book because I have about 300 stories already written. I could potentially put together at least three more books. Within seven days, God gave me five new stories. Didn't I tell you

He was working hard in my life? If you don't believe this, just try writing a story without His help.

When I began contacting bookstores, the owner of one shop asked how I decided to have it published. I explained that my oldest daughter is more computer savvy than I am; she researched, found Lulu.com and did the formatting, etc. for me. Now the book is on Amazon.com and *can* go out all over the world. After I told the owner all of this and more, he told me he had written a book many years ago, but never could afford to have it published; he is an older gentleman who decided he would look into publishing his book through the internet that very evening.

Because I am on disability, I called Social Security to find out how much money I could earn before it would affect my income. I talked with a young man who was as inquisitive as the guy in the previous paragraph. It seems he had written a children's book, but was unsure about publication. Now he has an idea and it seems God may use one book and one writer (me) to encourage publication of two other books. I certainly hope they will see God at work in this.

At Pandora's Bookshop in Lexington, only one person bought my book. She had seen in the advertisement that I also have myasthenia gravis, a progressive muscular weakness disease. Since business was slow in the extreme heat, we talked a long time, exchanged phone numbers, and email addresses, and have stayed in touch. So once again, I was reminded of what I once said about my book, "It's not all about money. It's about how I can share my love for the Lord with others."

This is one of my favorite scriptures from Second Corinthians 1:3-4: "Praise be to the God and Father of our Lord Jesus Christ, the Father of compassion and the God of all comfort, who comforts us in all our troubles, so that we can comfort those in any trouble with the comfort we ourselves received from God." So I give thanks to God for my new friend, Dorothy, and pray that God will heal her with a more level "playing field" that she might find the same remission I have experienced with this disease.

When I was signing books at the Bible Book Store in Salisbury, a young girl who loves gardening, opened the book automatically to "Thorns, Thistles, and Weeds." She just had to stand there reading the story. The owner kidded her saying, "You have to buy the book, if you want to read the stories." She said she didn't have any money, but she would come back later. I should have told her she could check My Sanctuary out at the Rowan Public Library Headquarters as I had donated one there. But I was so excited about all the nice compliments I had been receiving that I wasn't thinking straight.

Another customer that I remember from some years ago flipped through the book and asked me to sign it. As I was doing so, I suggested that she pass it along to friends with multiple sclerosis and/or other disabilities. She immediately remembered that her niece has MS so she asked me to sign a second book. God knows who will read this book, and He is working hard to be sure the book gets into the right hands.

My friend, Elaine, took five books to Corner Books and More in China Grove where she lives. One day she asked me if I would like to meet the bookstore owner. The lady said she was amazed that just the day before, a customer had asked her to sell some books on consignment. She had opened one called Rowan County Tales, and saw my name under the title on five stories. She realized then that I was the writer who would be there to sign books at the China Grove Farmer's Day.

Because the weather was predicting rain, "the other Linda" and I decided to postpone our meal. Well, it didn't rain and was a beautiful day, so I decided to ride my scooter across Brenner Avenue just as I did last year. I love the little community park by the railroad tracks and decided to sit in the shade to write a story that had been forming in my mind. As I sat in the shade writing, a tall nice looking man approached and asked me if I remembered him from the past. We worked together in Engineering at Celanese and I enjoyed talking about our past experiences. In the conversation, I discovered that he is not married, so something told me to ask him for a "date" if he was going to be free Saturday morning. (Me, ask a man for a "date;" only one other time in my life.) He said he had actually planned to "man a booth" at the China Grove Farmer's Day. I guess if I'd had false teeth, they might have fallen out in surprise.

I told him I needed a ride to and from, of all places, the China Grove Farmer's Day. Okay, if you are an unbeliever, you have my permission to call this a coincidence. (Fellow believers, you know that this is one more sample of God at work to get me where He wants me to be.) Three weeks later, I ran into him again.

While talking with the owner of the bookstore, I realized they also sell used books. I asked if she by any chance had Anne of Green Gables. When I first met "the other Linda" whom I mentioned earlier, we had decided we are *kindred spirits.* I remembered that phrase from this book about Anne and her friend. I discovered Linda has never read that book in all these years, so I had been planning to buy the book for her when I was out sometime. By now, you may have figured out the bookstore has had that book a long time, just waiting for the right buyer. (God tweaked my thoughts to remind me that a bookstore is the perfect place to find a consolidated book of three of the "Anne" stories. Duh!)

When I first purchased one hundred books, I placed five on consignment at three bookstores, and twenty at the Bible Bookstore. I knew Corner Books and More had sold two, because they had sent me a check for my share. As I looked around, I realized that there were more than three of my books in the store.

The night before at the bookstore in Salisbury, I was told that Ingram Distributors, a Christian distributing company, has bought some of my books from Lulu.com. The owner of the China Grove bookstore said several people had called during the week asking what time I would be there on Saturday. They had ordered some extras from Ingram so they would not run out. We sold several, but they still have copies of My Sanctuary. I encourage readers to give this book as a gift to those who are disabled, or have lost their soul mates.

When I was told that self-published books on the internet can *go all over the world* I continued to *think small*; not my stories I thought. I guess I had forgotten that I have an awesome BIG GOD, and my books can go wherever He sends them.

THE DISCOURAGING EVENTS

Okay, I'm frustrated now! And even a little discouraged. My multiple sclerosis exacerbation has confined me to a wheelchair since the fourth of July 2002. During my five weeks in the hospital and rehab, everyone thought I was so strong and brave. I kept telling them my emotions would crash after I came home and began to miss the things I used to do. Well, crash time has arrived.

What made things worse was dealing with a manual wheelchair. I should have insisted on a power chair from the beginning, even if I had to pay the complete cost. After several weeks of complaining, the power chair will soon be here and the insurance will pay all but twenty percent of it. It will be worth the debt to avoid the frustration I've had with the manual chair.

Some folks found it difficult to see how I could come home and live alone, but I was optimistic. (After all, I had just built my new handicapped accessible home.) Well, I discovered manual wheelchairs are for those who have someone to push them. When a patient has myasthenia gravis (a progressive muscle weakness disease) in addition to multiple sclerosis (a central nervous system disorder), it is very difficult to push oneself on new carpet.

(The suggestion of removing the carpet in a six-month old house was totally ridiculous.) The wheelchair has even marred the two small wood floor areas which is another source of my frustration.

I've gotten even more aggravated with the scars I've put on my new appliances. Marks on the walls and door facings cause me to become angry with myself. I had wide doorways, a large hall and bathroom put in, but yet I tend to accidentally hit corners. When that happens, I get discouraged.

Those who have been wheelchair confined know how difficult it is to come along beside of refrigerators, dishwashers, etc. Getting one's legs under desks and tables is often impossible. Fortunately, removing two of those eight chairs at my new dining room table has provided the best place for me to sit in the wheelchair. (And it is an ideal spot for watching the birds, and the construction of the other houses in the development.)

I had a ramp put at the side door so I would be able to get in and out in a wheelchair, but I've been too weak to push the chair up the ramp so mostly I've been confined inside the house except when someone is here to push me.

And that brings me to the greatest frustration. Being unable to come and go on my own as I have the past nine years has been discouraging. Although I have seldom ever been bored, I did have opportunities to get out more before. Now going out is a major movement for me, but also for those who are willing to take me places.

At the same point if I want the freedom I had before, I will have to buy a van with a lift and hand controls. That is a major expense and a difficult decision to make since I know MS can still cause further damage that may take away my driving capabilities totally in years to come.

The uncertainty of MS is probably one of the most frustrating things. I was told when this happened that I would never walk again, but I chose not to believe that, especially twenty-nine days later when my toes and feet showed some movement. Unfortunately, I still cannot lift my feet to walk. This is the point at which I have to accept confinement in a wheelchair. I really believe I can do so much better with a power chair, which will enable me to go outside alone. It will still be necessary to have a manual wheelchair with collapsible sides that will fold up for transporting. Perhaps then I will be able to call on others to take me out, rather than buying a van.

The one thing I miss the most is my water therapy, and I believe being in the water would help my legs. The problem is transportation to the club and getting in and out of the pool since I can't walk. Water therapy took a large chunk of my day before, so I now need to find some activity to fill those hours.

Tutoring a student, teaching Sunday school, and visiting various restaurants are other day trips I miss. But at least I can still read and write stories, and I know some who are less fortunate. When I feel too down, I remind myself of this and praise God for what I have left.

On one of my worse days, my friend, Gerri mailed me a devotional from Joni Eareckson Tada, a well-known Christian paraplegic. Joni has been greatly used by God right from her wheelchair. She refers to this episode in her life as "The Enemy's Strategy." Her faith here is based on Psalm 139. The next few paragraphs are in Joni's words – not mine:

> "This morning I was having a rough start getting out of bed. My paralysis was giving me fits. I shook my head and growled, "This body is a pain I hate...it."
>
> "Why was that so awful? Because the enemy has a deep hatred of my flesh and blood and all I was doing was agreeing with him. He gets a charge when I badmouth my

body and he would like to get you to do the same."

"Why? Because your body, even underneath wrinkles or fat, and despite the ravages of illness or old age is made in the image of God. Your heart, mind, hands, and feet are stamped with the imprint of the Creator – little wonder the devil wants you to be ashamed of your body!"

"This morning I had, once again, to plug my ears against the lies of the tempter and remember that I am 'fearfully and wonderfully made.' I rehearsed the old, familiar truth that God had a plan for this flesh and blood of mine and that is why the devil considers my body a threat – he understands that when I yield to God my body, all but paralyzed, my feet and hands are powerful weapons against his forces of darkness."

"The devil is only a fallen angel. He is a deceiver – He is doomed for destruction and until then, he has one goal in mind; your spiritual defeat, emotions malignant and physical frustration. If he tries to get you to agree with him today…don't."

Praise God for people like Joni who know what we need to read, and for friends like Geri, who knows when we need to listen.

THE DRESS

Well, let's see if I can remember all those things I wrote about…a story about "The Coat," "The Tray," and now "The Dress!" Yep, I surprised myself one day. I bought a dress…an expensive dress, reduced to a great bargain. For the first time in at least six years, I decided I wanted a new dress.

After the multiple sclerosis exacerbation in 2002, I gave most of my dresses away for several reasons. Partly, because I was gaining weight in the wheelchair and didn't expect they would ever fit again. All of those dresses were the longer length and I thought during that period of time while they were stylish, it would be nice for someone else to have them to wear, rather than for them to continue hanging in my closet.

I like to share my clothes with others who have a need, but I suppose the biggest reason was that I had become so cold-natured that even the thought of not having pants on made me shiver. On the other hand, I didn't think I would look very attractive, and the long dresses might get caught in the wheels of the chair.

I guess I had confined myself to being an invalid, mostly shut in my home. So why would I want a dress now? Once again, my life was changing. I had been using my walker and walked in and out of several restaurants, lost a few pounds, and even though I turned sixty that October, I felt younger, more attractive, and I wanted to be stylish again. I would not be able to wear high heels, which when worn with sheer hosiery, can flatter even my old legs. But even flat heel dress shoes looked better than bulky tennis shoes!

A new makeover with fresh colors, dressy clothes, good food and great company has led to nice evenings out from my little dollhouse. So far the new dress is hanging in the closet waiting for some warmer temperatures, but I can close my eyes and see myself as I once was. Once upon a time long, long ago, a teacher said we should restrict the number of times we use the words *I* and/or *Me.* Sorry folks, those words are what this story is all about…*I…I…I…me…me…me.*

OH, AND BEFORE THE SEASON WAS OVER, I PURCHASED TWO MORE DRESSES!

Psalm 30:11-12 reads: "You (God) turned my wailing into dancing; you removed my sackcloth and clothed me with joy that my heart may sing to you and not be silent. O Lord, my God, I will give you thanks forever."

THE FIRES IN OUR LIVES

My greatest fear has always been fire. I cringe when I hear about house or car fires and the burns the people may have to endure. So many times house fires result from smokers falling asleep with cigarettes, or children playing with matches. It's a good thing I don't smoke anymore, because I doze off to sleep so much easier these days.

As a child, I remember setting paper on fire with a magnifying glass on our concrete walkway. I was amazed how quickly the hot sunshine accomplished that. I recently bought my grandsons some magnifying glasses, but I don't plan to show them how to do that; they are much too curious.

We once owned a beautiful customized van called "The Silver Streak." One day I went to pick up my oldest daughter at a friend's house. I parked right outside their garage and got out to ring the doorbell. When I got back in and started the engine, I heard a "poof" sound and smoke started coming out from the dashboard.

I shut the engine off and we jumped out. Within minutes the flames were coming out from under the hood. By the time the fire department arrived, a lot of damage had been done. We were very fortunate that her friend's house and car were not damaged. Though the damage was extensive, our insurance covered the repairs, and we drove the van until my husband's death.

A couple years later, my daughter, Sonya, and I had enjoyed a nice day at the Fiber Industries Lake. She was just fifteen and driving her first car with a learner's permit. It was a little MG convertible and she was very excited to have a car almost like her sister's. As we were leaving the parking lot, I heard that familiar "poof" sound, but flames immediately began licking out at Sonya's feet.

She started screaming and trying to get away from the fire. She struggled with her seatbelt as she pulled her legs away from the immense heat. I panicked when her seatbelt wouldn't open and started trying to help her, but it held fast. Because she was so tiny and I guess had that adrenaline rush, she was able to wiggle out of the fastened seatbelt. Since the convertible top was down, she just shimmied out over the car door.

The car was slowing down and veering off the road. I was able to open my door and roll out into the grass. Because of my health problems, Sonya had to help me get up and we just stood there watching the MG burn completely up.

We had no way to call for help so by the time someone saw the smoke it was too late to save the car. Sonya ended up with a few burns on her feet that healed nicely, but a lasting fear of seatbelts is still with her. Needless to say, we both suffered our personal traumas. The thought of my beautiful young daughter burning in that fire still haunts me.

When I started driving again in 1995, I forced myself to start wearing a seatbelt, but Sonya still has panic attacks if she tries to wear one. Not long after the fire, we stopped to pick up a pizza one day. As she drove along and began to smell the warm pizza, she thought it was smoke that she smelled; she stopped the car in the middle of the street and jumped out. At that point, we realized the extreme trauma she had suffered.

It has been very difficult for Sonya to accept that her children have to wear seatbelts, and sometimes they question why they have to if Mommy doesn't. Sonya does have a doctor's excuse for not wearing one, but which is the greater danger?

I don't know, but I do remember the fear in her eyes when neither of us could get the belt unbuckled. The burns healed better than the emotional scars; I just pray that neither of us have to face fire again. Some folks choose to believe there is no fiery hell, but that belief disputes God's Word. Fortunately, as Christians, that is one fire we don't have to fear or worry about.

THE HAVE YOU EVERS...?

Do you ever have a day when it seems like nothing goes your way? Well folks, sometimes it seems I have a lot of those days. I reach for a glass with my grabber and either my hand relaxes too much, or I didn't have the instrument exactly right in my weak hand. I watch as that glass continues to fall, hits the floor, and explodes into hundreds of shards of glass all over my wooden floor.

Have you ever tried to clean up glass from a wheelchair when your broom and dustpan are several hundred feet from you? The slightest move puts glass in the tires and then glass gets transferred to the carpet.

Have you ever watched six cans of Cheerwine roll off the bar and hit the power chair and then the floor? Then you watch that cherry red drink erupt all over the floor, your pant legs, cabinets, etc.

Have you ever had to call a neighbor and ask them to come over to clean up your mess so you will not track the sticky drink everywhere; especially after you just spent a large sum of money having your carpet cleaned? Have you ever had to make that call at night when it's very cold and dark outside?

Have you ever been the neighbor that got that call and dropped everything to help your neighbor? In Matthew 22:37-40 Jesus said: “Love the Lord your God with all your heart and with all your soul and with all your mind." This is the first and greatest commandment. And the second is like it: ‘Love your neighbor as yourself.’ All the Law and the Prophets hang on these two commandments.”

Have you ever had to call a relative, friend, neighbor, or 911 to pick you up out of the floor or the yard? Have you ever been the receiver of that call and had to get dressed in the middle of the winter and go out in the rain to be a Good Samaritan?

The story of the Good Samaritan is preached in many churches and comes from Luke 10:30-37: A man was going down from Jerusalem to Jericho and fell into the hands of a robber. They stripped him of his clothes, beat him, and left him lying for dead. A priest and a Levi both passed on the other side without helping him. But a Samaritan passed by, stopped, poured oil and wine on his wounds and bandaged him. Then he put him on his donkey and carried him to the inn. He paid the innkeeper to look after him and promised to pay more if he needed.

Have you ever had to lie in the floor or on the ground, writhing in pain, waiting for help? Have you ever had to lay there thinking about the *foolish* move that caused the fall?

Have you ever had to wrestle with your thoughts, hoping that you can, did or will make the right decision? Jacob wrestled with God in Genesis 32:22-32. God touched the socket of Jacob's hip and his hip was wrenched; he then limped because of his hip. But God blessed him and allowed Jacob to see him "face to face," and yet spared his life.

Sometimes I feel like I have wrestled with God over some issues or some scripture that I may not completely understand. Because of multiple sclerosis, I cannot walk without a limp, but I've learned from reading God's word that He had a purpose for my health problems. The purpose of my *limp, weakness,* and other issues has given me subject matter in my speaking and writing; these problems have been so that I can give God the glory for seeing me through all of these events in my life.

Have you ever had to live with having made wrong choices or decisions? Maybe you made a bad legal decision that caused you to end up in a "prison-like state with bars."

Maybe God has plans to use you just as He used Paul and Silas when they were in chains in prison. (Acts

16:22-40) God sent a violent earthquake that caused the prison doors to open and the chains to come loose. Seeing the power of God and experiencing the witness of Paul and Silas, the jailer and his family were saved and the disciples were released.

If in our mistakes, our bondage, or our sin, we manage to bring even one person to the salvation experience, God will bless us. If pain, sorrow, or loss, has us in prison, God can release us from those "chains or bars" if we ask Him to give us peace and acceptance of our situation.

Have you ever had to face the loss of your soul mate, one of your children, or parents? When I was a child, it seemed we were always going to funerals. My first real loss was my grandfather the summer before my senior year in high school. Other than my Father God, I never knew my *real* father.

Then I lost my grandmother, my mother, my older brother, my husband and various aunts and uncles. Sometimes now at age 61, I see so many folks younger than me dying.

Have they ever invited Christ into their heart? Have you ever…done so? If not, pray about it now; tomorrow may be too late.

THE HISTORY OF THE SCOOTERS

This story began in 1993 in the parking lot at Holly Leaf Apartments. Some folks who knew me during this chapter of my life may remember parts of this, but new readers may not. My husband died in February 1993 and in May, I moved into an apartment at the edge of town. I had sold our waterbed because of my bad health, and ordered a single hospital bed to be delivered the day I moved.

When the guys came with the bed, they also set a three-wheel scooter off in the parking lot. I told them I had not ordered that, and they said it was just for me to experiment with while they put the bed together.

At that time the color mauve was very popular and with one spin around, I fell in love with my scooter. Since I was unable to drive back then, the scooter was answered prayer. The scripture says that when we don't know how to pray, the Holy Spirit hears the *groanings* of our heart and prays for us. The Lord knew what I needed and wanted before I had any way of knowing the blessing of owning a scooter, rather than having to depend on someone to push me in a wheelchair.

I immediately told the fellows that I wanted to buy the scooter that day. They protested that it was their new demo model, and rather expensive. After some lengthy discussion, they called the home office and told the lady about this *crazy woman* who was insisting they accept a check and leave the scooter.

I got on the phone with the lady and discussed my situation. She explained that the scooter was very expensive, and that I might get help with the cost from my insurance company, if I would be patient and wait. I told her I had just sold everything I owned and would write a check that day, if she would accept it. After much pleading, she told the men to leave the scooter.

I was still insured by my husband's *catastrophic* insurance plan and within a short period of time, they paid for the scooter and my money was returned to me. The scooter became my transportation to the mall, the grocery and drug stores, and several restaurants for lonely meals that sure beat eating alone in that small apartment.

But most important, it enabled me to ride back and forth to the apartment pool where I discovered water aerobics; the best atmosphere in which to get used to living alone. During the following years, it became my *toy* that enabled me to ride my two grandsons around for different activities. There are so many precious memories about those days, and they became the *boy stories* that some folks have enjoyed reading.

We all talk about how time flies and before I knew it, and after many miles of wear and tear, the scooter was "on its last leg." After nine years, the cost of scooters has come down some, but my health had improved and I didn't need one as badly in 2002 when I first moved into my new home.

By then I had been driving for several years and only used the scooter for long distance walking, so I parked it on my back porch and used my rolling walker to get to and from my car. Then in July, I had the multiple sclerosis exacerbation that took away my ability to walk.

A little over a month later, one of my readers brought a used scooter and a lightweight wheelchair to my home because he no longer needed those. I offered to pay him, but he wanted to give both items to me. I felt so blessed! (Another one of those times when unspoken prayer was answered.)

Two days later, I got a call from the medical supply store telling me that someone had come in, and purchased a new scooter for me that would be delivered at my convenience. A few hours later, he arrived with two scooters (a red one and a blue one.) I was given my choice of colors, and he told me the purchaser wished to remain anonymous.

I was absolutely stunned that someone would spend that much money on a gift for me. He said they told him they had enjoyed my stories over the years, and just wanted to donate this. I told him someone had given me a used one, and I wasn't sure what to do. He said the new one was paid for, and he couldn't take it back.

After thinking about this for several days, I advertised my old scooter "free as is" and it was picked up within hours after the paper was printed. Finally, I called the giver of the first gift, and explained I now had two scooters in my little house. They were both too nice to leave outside, and I wanted him to decide what I should do with the scooter he had given me.

I suppose I could have given it to someone else or sold it, but it just didn't seem right to do that. I had been twice blessed and thought he might know someone else to bless.

I am still amazed and thankful for all the blessings I have received. My family, friends, and other readers continue to bless me. I do believe that God has had his hand in all these events and his timing has been perfect for my needs. God is so good to me!

THE *I CANS* AND *I CAN'TS*

"I think I can! I think I can!" How many times did I read the story about the little engine to my daughters and grandsons? And hopefully in future years, I will be able to read the same little book to my granddaughter, Hallie Renee.

I've always encouraged my kids to think positive, and I believe I am a positive thinker. But the reality is that we all live with some things we *can* do and some things we *can't*. Those with health problems may be presented with more of the negatives than the positives, but this is the stage at which our attitudes play an important part in our lives.

I decided if I were to make a comparison list of my *cans* and *cant's* it might inspire me and maybe others as well; so here goes:

I *can* fall at my washing machine (3 times in 2 years), but I *can't* get myself up. In fact, I *can't* get myself up anywhere I fall, but I *can* depend on so many people to help me; and I thank everyone who ever has.

I *can't* sing, but I *can* listen to music, and I'm so thankful for my hearing. Even though I don't hear as well as I used to, I *can* hear better than those who are deaf.

I *can* see the natural beauty all around me, though I *can't* do much to preserve it. But I *can* see and some people *can't*.

I *can* drive with my hand controls, even though I *can't* travel like I used to. There are some people who *can't* leave their homes at all.

From my wheelchair I *can* sweep and mop my tiny kitchen and entranceway floor and the bathroom, even though I *can't* vacuum my carpet.

Most times I "*can*" walk in and out of the pool now with great effort, though I still "*can't*" walk out of the hot tub. But, hey, at first I had to use the lift to get in and out of both.

I *can* only swim about thirty minutes now, as compared to more than an hour before this multiple sclerosis exacerbation, but I *can't* complain, because in 2002 I was told I wouldn't be able to swim or float anymore at all.

I *can* put my thoughts on paper, even though it seems I *can't* write much without reference to multiple sclerosis, but that's my life now. I might as well confront it and share with others. In Matthew 5:14 Jesus said, "You are the light of the world. A city on a hill cannot be hidden. Neither do people light a lamp and put it under a bowl.

Instead they put it on its stand and it gives light to everyone in the house. In the same way, let your light shine before men that they may see your good deeds and praise your father in heaven."

Instead of sliding on a board, I *can* stand now to make most of my transfers, but I *can't* remain standing too long. However, I will never forget the first day of rising to a standing position after five months of being unable to do so.

I *can* do a little container gardening from my wheelchair even though I *can't* have the beautiful yard I once had.

I could probably continue on with the comparisons indefinitely but I expect ya'll are beginning to see how this applies in your own lives. So, is your glass "half-full" or "half-empty?" Do you spend too much time daily thinking about the *can'ts* rather than thanking God for the things you *can* do?

I *can* encourage others to love the Lord, and study the Bible, but I *can't* make anyone accept Jesus Christ as their Savior. I *can* pray for the salvation of others, but the Holy Spirit has to speak to their hearts and I *can't* control this.

Let me just stop here so each of you *can* examine your own *cans* and *cannots*.

THE JEWELRY

Over the years I've written about *the coat, the dress, the robe,* and after this special day, I decided it was time to write about *The Jewelry.* I'm sure most of you ladies love jewelry, and some men like to give jewelry as a gift for special occasions.

I never had any special jewelry as a child; the first jewelry I received as a gift was a watch. It was a Christmas present from a special boyfriend when I was 15. That watch is still tucked away in my jewelry box with many fond memories. It was so pretty and dainty that these old eyes can no longer read the numbers.

When my husband proposed to me, he gave me a tiny diamond that was surrounded with a square setting that somewhat smothered the stone because it was white gold (which was my favorite back then). Joe was working hard for only $30 a week and we moved to Indiana where he could make more working for his brother. He had purchased the ring on credit, and as soon as we got it and his car paid off, we came back to North Carolina.

I don't remember receiving many compliments through the years, but I loved my ring and my husband. After Joe passed away 27 years later, the engagement ring band had worn very thin and the diamond needed resetting. The owners of Signature Jewelry went to my church, and Patsy helped me pick a stylish setting in yellow gold. I changed the ring to my index finger and quit wearing my wedding band. Since that time I've received many compliments on my little diamond almost everywhere I go, especially if I "reach out to touch" someone or something. Experts tell us that diamonds appreciate in value, and others say diamonds are "a girl's best friend." I know my appreciation grows every time I receive a compliment on my little jewel.

I never asked for jewelry because we always needed other things more through the years. Sometimes I would buy costume jewelry, but never anything expensive. For our 25th wedding anniversary, we had planned to go out West, but in April of that year I had seizures, and we had to postpone our trip. My husband surprised me with a short sterling silver chain that has a wedding bell surrounded by a wedding ring. He had it especially designed for me, and I've never seen anything quite like it. I've always treasured this, but seldom wear necklaces unless I can slip the chain over my head. I no longer have anyone to fasten the clasp for me, so I wear necklaces less and less.

By now some of you are probably wondering why I'm writing about this. Well, remember I've said before, I started out writing my stories years ago in a journal and then began to share them with others, so just consider this one of those journal entries.

The day before this story came to my mind, I had been browsing around in an antique shop downtown. I was not in the buying mode until I saw a beautiful white embroidered blouse that only cost $8. It was my size and was from Honolulu, so I couldn't resist. Then I saw a rack of tops where each one was less than $10. There were three I wanted to wear with some pants I have.

Later as I was preparing to go out with some friends, the neckline of one top and some silver hoop earrings cried out for a short necklace. For the first time in over 16 years, I realized this necklace would fit perfectly if my girlfriend would fasten it. I looked in the mirror and actually felt attractive. All day and into the evening, I toyed with the necklace and sweet memories of the love of my life.

Joe only brought me nice jewelry one other time, but once again, had it custom made for me. He knew how I loved crosses so he had a set of earrings made with crosses that had a tiny sliver of a diamond in the center of the cross.

I loved those earrings and wore them almost everywhere I went.

One day when I got out on my side of the car at his mother's house, I realized one cross was missing. I was so upset; we checked all over the ground, in the car, and our house when we returned home. I was heartbroken and Joe assured me that he could get another earring to match the one that I still had; and so he did.

Just about a year later, I drove us to Joe's old home place. Just as he got out on the passenger side of the car, I saw him bend over and pick something up. We all called him "Eagle-eye Joe" because he could spot things on the side of the road at 70 miles an hour. When he stood up he asked, "Babe, have you lost an earring lately?"

"I don't think so," I replied. He had a big grin on his face and replied, "I believe you did once upon a time."

Joe walked around the car and said, "Close your eyes and open your hand." I felt the excitement rising as he squeezed my hand closed. When I opened my eyes, I was shocked to see that he had found the lost cross earring.

The only damage was that the post which the jeweler had put on the cross had been broken off. To look at it, one would never have believed it had been in that gravel driveway for over a year. As it happened, they had just put new gravel down and the process of doing so must have uprooted the earring. Joe took that one back and had it fixed on a chain. I ended up with three crosses and wore them frequently; until he was no longer there to fasten the tiny chain.

My health was so bad then that I gave the set to my youngest daughter. When I see her with the jewelry on now, memories wash over me just as they did this time over the anniversary necklace. Sometimes, I'm tempted to use my ancestral rights and become an "Indian giver." But she has memories of her dad also, and I believe the gift has been special to her.

Joe has been gone now a little over sixteen years, and days like this one bring him back to me in a vivid way. With a little help, or by watching my hands in the mirror, that old necklace that he had created for me may be new to me all over again.

Memories of my husband and the jewelry he gave me reminded me of some scripture that got me through my early years as a widow and it reads like this:

> Ecclesiastes 3:1-4 "There is a time for everything and a season for every activity under heaven;...a time to weep and a time to

laugh, a time to mourn and a time to dance…"

THE LADY AND THE SLIPPER

When I was a child, I wore a lot of hand-me-downs like so many others of my generation. The shoes that I remember most were those old heavy black and white saddle oxfords. Some of the more expensive ones were made out of soft leather and didn't look as bulky as the cheap ones I had to wear.

There were some times when we had to insert cardboard to make those shoes fit better, but we knew better than to complain because when school started, we usually got one new pair of shoes.

In the summer we went barefoot, except to church. Most other days, we still wore our school shoes. Once in awhile, someone gave us summer shoes.

When I was a senior in high school, I got a job uptown in the Diana Shop. I bought myself a two-piece wool suit with flecks of red on a brown background. When the girl from Stanley County sang about her red high heels, I remembered my first pair of red patent spike heels that I purchased to match that suit. Boy, I guess I thought I was the stuff until after I got married and gained a few pounds.

After I started having health problems, wearing spike heels was one of many things I had to give up. I loved to wear the sandals that one could just slip one's foot right under the front strap. I guess I always liked wearing sandals because even now, at age 61, I'm often told how attractive my feet are; what a delight for one who is in a wheelchair or on a scooter.

But now my feet slide off the sides of that style of shoes so that too is a thing of the past. The only other shoe style I like so much is a pair of gold sandals with a slight heel that I can still wear if I stay in my wheelchair.

I guess the reason I liked those shoes so much was because I wore them when I was a teacher in a singles Sunday school class about eight years ago and one of the young adult males told the whole class how beautiful the shoes were and what pretty feet I have. I was the oldest single lady in the group and I sure appreciated that compliment. Those are the only dress shoes I've kept in my closet since this major multiple sclerosis exacerbation in 2002. I just couldn't bear to give them away as they are still like new and very stylish.

So at this point, readers are probably thinking...ho hum...where did this story come from and what's the point? Read on...

My daughters used to wear ballet slippers and I always thought they looked so comfortable, but I never took dance so I had never owned any like this. I found a pair of shoes that are quite similar to ballet slippers, except the big toe is cut out. They felt so soft to the touch, so I thought they would be very comfortable. (Because of the effects MS has on my feet, I can't stand stiff leather shoes on my feet now; certainly not like those old stiff oxfords.)

Due to the fine soft leather, these slippers were more expensive than I would usually pay but after six years of tennis shoes, I couldn't resist. Unfortunately sometimes when my feet swell, the little elastic band becomes uncomfortable to my sensitive feet. When that happens, I usually take the slippers off and either leave them on the floorboard of my scooter or put them in the basket as I ride from one place to another.

Well, one day when traveling from Point A to Point B, I found myself missing one slipper. I had to get the disability van to return to the hospital to see if I had dropped it along the way. Fortunately, it was at the front desk waiting for this old lady to return. A young man found the slipper out in the courtyard where I had went to see the pansies. He returned it to the desk as he figured someone would be anxious to find that new shoe. He certainly had no idea how desperately this lady wanted to find her new slipper. I thought of Cinderella when she lost her glass slipper and gave thanks to God for the young man who took the time to return the leather slipper to the receptionist's desk, and to the ladies there who were holding my little slipper for me.

THE LOVE OF MY LIFE

Forty-four years ago when this was a safer time to meet strangers, teenagers cruised through our little town with the windows down, music blasting, and just having fun.

One day my girlfriend, Sandy, and I stopped in a line at a red light. One guy in the car next to us said, "I sure would like to ride in a black Mercury." Sandy said, "Get in." I couldn't believe that country boy got out and jumped in the back seat just as the light turned green.

He and my friend joked back and forth as we dragged through town until it was time for us to go home. I was very shy (nobody believes that now) and mostly just listened and occasionally turned to smile at his corny jokes.

He called my friend that night and asked her to convince me to go out with him. Why me? Later he claimed that he fell in love with me as he watched the sunlight sparkle red highlights through the back of my long auburn hair.

We were married two weeks after I graduated from high school when I was only seventeen, and we honored our vows until his death parted us when he was only forty–seven years old.

Though age, medications and poor health has dulled the sparkle in my hair, Joe would be pleased that the only other change is a few silver strands. At age sixty-two, some folks find it hard to believe I have never put any color or bleach on my hair. I've even had issues when ladies have accused me of lying about that. But why would I color my hair? After all, this color did help me catch the love of my life!

THE MAGIC SCARF

Sometimes a special item comes into our lives and when this happens to me, I like to tell others about it. Some readers might remember my stories about the coat, the tray, the house, etc.

Recently my oldest daughter gave me a new scarf. It's called a magic scarf because one can wear it as a sash, a hat, hood, poncho, or as a cowl neck over a sweater. It resembles the feather boas from the days of yesteryear.

This is the warmest scarf I've ever worn. It's not wool, but it is soft and fluffy and one hundred percent polyester. It reminds me of those fluffy little dogs whose eyes get lost in their fur.

Every time I've worn this scarf someone ask where they might buy one. These scarves are found in several different places and most cost between five and ten dollars. They are available in many different colors.

The biggest reason I like this scarf is because it is so very warm even though it is light weight. When used as a hood, it doesn't mess up one's hairstyle which is really nice on the way to church.

I am a very cold-natured person and have owned several woolen scarves, but seldom wore them. Those generally made me itch if I put them snugly against my skin. The magic scarf is so soft and warm that I've had visions of taking it with me when I go into the air-conditioned church. (I know, I know that might be a bit tacky with summer clothes, but as cold as I get it might be worth the laughs.)

A friend was traveling out of state and came across these scarves in many colors, so she purchased a purple one for me. The way folks admired my black one, I'm sure they will be impressed with my purple one, even if I wear it with my spring clothes.

The nice ladies at the hospital compliment me on my color coordination and I have several friends to thank. So thanks to all!

THE PAST SEVEN YEARS

Has it really been seven years since the major multiple sclerosis attack took so much away from me? Well, as of July 4th and 5th it was. In some ways it seems so terribly long ago. But when I review all that has happened during the healing period, I am amazed how quickly time has flown by.

At first, the days were long and drawn out as I came to terms with how my abilities had been affected. Nights were spent wrestling with negative thoughts as I tried to plan for the future. Days were spent in therapy learning to adjust to my limitations.

From time to time, folks continue to ask me what happened on that hot summer morning, so here is a short update. I had only been in my little doll house four months and was still in the process of stocking the pantry and purchasing other household items.

That particular morning was so unusually hot, and when I returned home I had several trips to make from the car. I got tired and weak as I pushed the loaded walker up the ramp.

As soon as I got the refrigerated items put away, I crashed until my family came by to make ice cream. By evening, I was so weak that I knew my physical condition was going downhill rapidly. Because of the holiday, I decided to sleep at home in case the emergency room was overflowing.

Early the next morning, my oldest daughter helped me get ready and drove me to the hospital. As I tried to get out of the car, my legs gave way and I went down in the parking lot. For the following five months, I was unable to rise again.

The next day I was told I would never be able to walk, swim, float, or drive. After several days of IV steroids, I was moved to rehab where I stayed for five weeks. I had lost control of almost everything from my breast down.

Most of this has been written about in various ways in separate articles but many people who discover they have multiple sclerosis want to hear more. Many folks have been encouraged to see the progress I have made.

I considered myself blessed that after about five months, I was able to rise to a standing position and even take a few steps with a walker. Eventually, I became able to walk in and out of the pool at the YMCA, and do many of the same water aerobics that I had done before this major exacerbation had happened.

My real purpose in writing this article was not to rehash everything I've been through. I was thinking more about the passage of time. During this time, the Lord blessed me with a granddaughter, several new friends, a new hobby and so many other blessings. Kids I know are graduating from college, high school, and advancing to middle school and beyond. Some are getting married and others are having babies.

My daughters are now in their thirties and forties, and I now qualify as a senior citizen. My hair is getting a few silver strands, and my body sags more all the time. I don't mind so much that my looks are failing, but *senior moments* are one thing I could do without. It seems confusion and forgetfulness is the result of medication which itself is one of the biggest problems in my life these days.

In the past since I had no insurance coverage for drugs, the cost of the medication kept me on a tight budget. The side effects are most unpleasant. Dry mouth and drowsiness have become a daily part of my life.

This forgetfulness was particularly alarming just recently when I set my microwave for twenty minutes instead of two. Then I went off and forgot about it until about six minutes later when I smelled burnt bacon. I ruined my three-year-old microwave and my grandson's breakfast. The purchase of a new microwave took a small chunk out of my monthly budget, but I was so thankful I found it before it caught on fire.

I kept dozing off to sleep as I tried to write this story and got confused and frustrated as I typed on the computer. My cursive writing has gotten so sloppy and I've been amazed that I can make the greeting cards (my new hobby).

In spite of my physical limitations, I'm thankful God has given me more time here with my family and friends. I know He may have more plans for me and when my time is up here, I will be ready to go to my heavenly home with a new body.

THE PETS IN OUR LIVES

"No pets allowed." That's what my folks said when I was a child. When I got married, my husband wanted to give me something I had never had: a dog. We took that little puppy to our new home in Indiana and during the day, it often eased my homesickness. We had to keep the little dog on a chain because our house was crammed between the road and the train track.

That was over forty-four years ago and I don't even remember the dog's name, or what eventually happened to him. The one thing I do remember is that dog wouldn't even eat the results of my first attempt at making a red velvet cake (one of my favorite cakes.) Red cake coloring was difficult to locate out in the county where we lived, and I had gone to a lot of trouble to get all the ingredients together. When the cake failed, I was sick at heart and tossed it out to the dog. At that time, I assumed dogs would eat anything, but I guess I didn't realize how bad the cake really tasted.

We had numerous dogs after we moved back to North Carolina, but I don't remember the names or the order of most of them. We had a variety of breeds; there were German Shepherds, Irish Setters, Eskimo Spitz,

Collies, and several of the Heinz 57 variety. Some of our dogs bring back special memories like the one who wouldn't eat the cake.

Ginger was half of one and half of another kind, but she was very special because one time she stood her ground between my daughter and a snake. Sherry was just a toddler and sometimes she would venture into the front yard in the direction of the road. Ginger would prance between her and the road, barking profusely. If Sherry didn't come when we called her, Ginger would gently push her down on the ground.

Unfortunately, Ginger ventured across the road herself one day; those were the days before leash laws, and we had a large yard. I called her to come back, and she was hit by a car driven by my husband's sister, of all people. Sherry was broken-hearted and I felt really guilty because had I not called her, she may have come back when it was safer. Once we had a party-mix cocker spaniel. She was bred to a golden male and we had a litter of valuable puppies. One day we came home and found the puppies trying to nurse the mother who was dead. Evidently, someone hunting on or near our farm had shot her. She barely made it back to her puppies.

My husband went to the pound and got a big black stray mama dog who adopted the puppies. Watching those gold and white spotted puppies nurse that big black dog was something to see. Later the black dog mysteriously disappeared, and we never could find her. One day, we saw a picture of a very rare breed of dogs that looked just like her. This was during a period of time when a lot of dogs were being stolen and we often wondered if someone recognized her as an expensive dog that they could sell.

We kept one of the golden cockers and became attached enough to him that I made my first attempt at raising a house dog. One night while we were away, he decided to paw through the new flooring at our kitchen door. We had to cut a section out from under our refrigerator to replace the part he ruined in our home.

Then there was the day he scratched the slats on our louvered doors between the kitchen and living room. I then decided that he had to move back outdoors. One afternoon while I napped, I had chained him to the post on our carport. When I awoke, I found that he had tried to jump off the carport and hanged himself. I was devastated and again felt so guilty.

After several years, we were finally able to build some nice kennels and we decided to breed collies. We ended up with three gorgeous collies that were the sweetest, most affectionate dogs we ever owned. One day Prince got so excited when I entered the kennel that he jumped and hit his head on the low opening door to the lot. I believe he actually *saw stars.* He lost his vision in one eye, but continued to show the same exuberance throughout his life.

After my husband died, I had to find new owners, as I could no longer take care of my collies. One of our best friends took Prince, so I was able to visit him from time to time until he died of old age. He is the only one that I know for sure ended up with a good home, and a happy carefree life.

Some people encouraged me to get a house pet after I moved to my apartment. I tried a bird for awhile, but it was too noisy. I had several quiet fish, but they died early deaths. I'm not really a cat woman though I always appreciated that our many outdoor cats kept mice and snakes away from our farm house. I might enjoy having an outdoor cat now, if it wouldn't hang around my back door; and if it could keep some of these pesky rabbits away.

When our daughters were young, we had rabbits, goats, peacocks, guineas, cows and horses. I usually ended up with the associated chores and animals are expensive, so these days I just say, "No thanks, no pets allowed."

THE PRINCESS AND THE PEA

Sometimes I feel like the princess from the story "The Princess and the Pea." Some of you may remember the fairy tale about the princess who could feel the tiny pea through a high stack of mattresses. (I bet I got your attention.)

When one sits in a wheelchair so much of the time, one tends to be extremely conscious of the seat of the chair. Every little crumb and every wrinkle in the cushion or in one's clothes causes some discomfort. Somehow when one is cooking or eating in a wheelchair, crumbs have a way of ending up in the seat. Handicapped people are told in therapy to change positions in the wheelchair every fifteen minutes to avoid bed sores so I guess the position of the crumbs changes also.

My derriere has been one of my most worrisome body parts since I had this major exacerbation in 2002. I had attributed the burning sensation to the multiple sclerosis and resigned myself to there being no cure. At times I've had to lie on my side to withstand the discomfort.

When I finally went to my family doctor, he thought it might be a fungal infection caused by moisture from perspiration. Imagine my delight after all this time when I discovered "Lotrimin," an antifungal powder which is providing some relief. Yes, this is another one of those "almost too personal stories," but perhaps it is an answer for some readers who are having similar problems.

Thinking of fairy tales, I've also been a lot like Goldilocks in "The Three Bears." I've tried three cushions, three pads and at least three different positions in bed just as she tried different chairs and beds. (I haven't had any problem deciding which food to eat.)

Many of us have similar problems and some have discovered solutions while others have not. I like to read the doctor's column in the paper because I find some answers there. He has a long running controversial article about what will help fungus of one's toenails. Some readers have found that using *Vick's Vaporub* on one's toenails helps clear this up. The argument is on going, but I have found that it has helped my toenails. (Now, my problem is not as severe as some folks but perhaps it will just take longer continual use by others.)

Then there is the common problem of ringing in the ears. My girls often think I have *selective hearing,* but this is one problem I would never *select.* My worse time with this is when I lie down at night when things are so quiet.

My answer to this has been listening to a CD with the sounds of the ocean flowing throughout the room. During the day I like for things to be quiet, but I have started listening to Christian music to drown out other noises I don't want to hear. Yeah, I guess that is *selective* hearing, but the music puts me in a praise and worship mood rather than a frustrated angry mood.

Those who have MS should never assume every problem is due to the disease itself though it may be causing other problems. Sometimes if we can afford it, medicine works with our health problems.

Well, these problems are like the pea in the princess' bed. It's time for this princess to retire for the night.

THE PUTTING OF ACTION BEHIND OUR FAITH

Recently, I wrote a story about finding favor with the Lord through our faith. Right after that I heard a sermon about “Putting Action Behind our Faith.” The pastor’s first question was about whether we are showing our faith in our lives today.

His first example was from the scripture located in Mark 2:1-12, “Jesus Heals a Paralytic.” That has been one of my favorite Bible stories, possibly because of my disability. I’m not sure why this subject is not preached on as much as some others, unless it is because less people are crippled (handicapped, today’s terminology). But just as in most all scriptures, the importance is more in the paralytic’s faith than it is in his paralysis.

He had enough faith to ask some friends to carry him to see Jesus. The preacher made some comments that weren’t spelled out in scripture, but certainly are appropriate. Have you ever wondered how much the paralytic weighed? When the major attack took my ability to walk in 2002, it was difficult to keep my weight down. I’m sure I would have been quite heavy to have been carried on a mat to church. And how far did the sick man live from Capernaum? I expect these four friends were probably very tired by the time they got to the house where Jesus was. Have we ever thought about how back-breaking the effort was to lift the sick man to the roof after carrying him the distance? And then they had to work to put a hole in the roof so they could lower him into the room where Jesus was speaking.

I know it is very difficult for some folks to load and unload me to go to church, and they don't have to carry me the distance. In years past, most churches did not have elevators. I know that is discouraging to handicapped people and is one of the reasons there are so many *shut-ins.* The other reason is lack of transportation. I understand the reasons people don't offer to take me back and forth to church "every time the doors are open" as my brother, Michael, did when he was able.

But it was different in Jesus' time when everyone walked. In some parts of the world, some walking still takes place today. If it were not for Joni Eareckson Tada and her "Wheels for the World" program, some paralytics would have no wheelchairs. Joni certainly has "put action behind her faith" which has resulted in a lot of faith-based prayers being answered. (If you have extra wheelchairs, put your action behind you faith and pass them on to those who need them.)

The other point I find interesting in this Bible story is that all Jesus had to do was "see their faith" and he said to the paralytic, "Son, your sins are forgiven." Because of the action of the audience, Jesus told the paralytic, "I tell you, get up, take your mat, and go home." He walked out in the full view of everyone and they were amazed.

This part of the scripture reminded me of the five months in 2002 when I couldn't walk. An "angel" sent me a pin that read, "Expect a Miracle." I put my faith in God and after much effort, finally stood on my feet. Because of my faith, God enabled me to walk some with a walker. I know that God could say to me, "Get up and walk normal again." But I also know that isn't necessarily his plan for me. Jesus healed the paralytic then, to show the authority the Son of Man had.

I once attended a Bible study (by video) presented by the now-famous Beth Moore. Once again, some scripture that I had read many times suddenly spoke to my heart in a new way, and I know that God has used me through my speaking and writing to serve others. This scripture is from Isaiah 61:1&2 and Beth pointed out how it applied in her life, and God got my attention:

"The spirit of the Sovereign Lord is on me,
because the Lord has anointed me to preach

good news to the poor. He has sent me to bind up the brokenhearted, to proclaim freedom for the captives and release from darkness for the prisoners, to proclaim the year of the Lord's favor and the day of vengeance of our God, to comfort all who mourn…"

And if you question why I can see myself here, I will finish with a rewarding message that was left on my answering machine by a troubled person who had bought three of my books:

"Linda, I just had to tell you. I just reread your book today and it is pulling me out of a deep hole. You really did do it, young lady. I appreciate your book every time I read it. It does get better and better. Thank you! You don't have to call me back. If it gets too rough, I'll just reread your book again!"

And to those of you who are already telling me I need to write another book, I just want you to know God is at work telling me the same thing since He gave me two stories today. Give God the Glory!

THE REASON, THE SEASON, OR THE LIFETIME

I'm learning more and more about God's timing. I've been getting a lot of emails and they seem to come just when I need them most. It's strange, too, how they often correspond with preachers I've listened to, and notes I've taken over the past year.

One page of notes was under a title called "Stepping into Your Destiny." I took this message and applied it to my own life. Perhaps you can do the same with these notes by putting your name where "I" talk about "myself."

"I" am what God wanted "me" to be…God brings people into "my" life and then sometimes He moves them out. Sometimes these people are *crutches* that "I" need to quit using, or being used by them. If someone walks away, "I" shouldn't ask them to stay.

The preacher likes to add some humor and he said "I" shouldn't hold on to a dead horse; "I" should dismount and walk away. He went on to say that when God is through with something, no amount of *super glue* will hold it together. Another interesting comment was that "I" should let the *wrong* people go out of my life, and God will bring *new* ones into my life. I know that has happened through the years; friends come and go for different reasons. When a season is over, things change.

Another humorous comment was made about where "I" am in my life, and where God wants "me" to be. It's a bit of a challenge, but the pastor said, "Don't settle for the side streets…move on to the freeways." "I'm" not too crazy about *driving* on the interstate, but if it is God's will, "I" will be on the road sharing His Word wherever and whenever it is in His plan. The preacher said that "I" should let go of those who hold me back, or "I" cannot fulfill "my" destiny.

Another note "I" came across said that where "I" am, is not where "I'm" supposed to stay. "I" cannot allow myself to become discouraged, now is not the time for that. My blessings are God's favor. "I've" walked in His blessing, but "I" have this feeling in "my" heart that it has been a fraction of the future blessings He has for "me." God is able; He is a God of increase. According to the pastor, what God has done in "my" past can "pale" compared to my future.

"I've" decided to get excited about "my" future, in spite of "my" disability. "My" destiny is determined by God. He has and He will bring people into my life to help me. "I've" decided in spite of risks, "I" will not settle where "I" am. The preacher said, "You've been where you are long enough. It's time to go beyond where you are now." "I" must "get out of my rut" and be ready for a whole new season, and a new vision of the abundant overflowing life God has in store for "me."

Sometimes "I've" allowed disability and the thoughts and advice of others to limit my mindset. God can change our minds, if we allow him to. If we want to be hard nosed and stubborn, then He might choose not to use us. "I" must have faith that this may be "my" year to expect increase in "my" life, so that "I" can share that increase with others.

Do not misunderstand, "I" am not talking about financial increase..."I'm" referring to *my usefulness* to reach others for our Lord and Savior.

Some folks already think "I" take too many risks, but "I" heard a preacher say today that Christians through the centuries have suffered for the Lord. If "I" suffer, "I" suffer...God knows "my" heart. In spite of "my" mistakes, "my" sins, and "my" failures, He knows it is "my" desire to serve Him by helping others come to know Him, even in their worse times of stress and suffering.

"I've" suffered in different ways most of "my" life, but "I'm" fully aware that many suffer worse every day.

“I’” do believe that reading God’s word, and accepting Jesus Christ as “my” Savior, has given me a peace that many people with health problems have not yet found. “I” can only pray that because God keeps giving me stories to write, and people to reach, that “I” can reach those He desires “me” to reach.

Did you put yourself in the places that “I” was in?

THE ROBE

There were the stories about the doll house, the coat, the tray and now this is another "item" story about "The Robe." Just as I was about "The Coat," I'm somewhat ashamed to admit what I paid for "The Robe." But my daughter reminded me that I've worn the coat since 1996 and it still looks stylish and is in great shape for one that is winter white and was worn every winter until I became wheelchair confined.

Well, this story is about "the robe." Sherry and I went to Merle Norman's for their spring sale and a makeover. As it turned out, both my daughters' birthdays were approaching and they were each low on makeup so I ended up buying early presents for them as well as a couple of makeup items for myself. (My skin certainly needs all the help it can get due to age and many years of sun exposure.)

Ladies who shop at Merle Norman's know how makeovers require some extra time and the longer we were there, the colder I got. The owner overheard me tell Sherry that we would soon have to leave because I was so cold. She offered to get a robe from the spa to see if that would help me warm up. Those of you who know how cold-natured I am understand how much I appreciated that.

The owner came out with a beautiful plush-looking robe and after a few minutes of having it over my legs, I could feel the warmth. I decided to stand up and put it on and immediately I was "in love." I believe this robe is the softest warmest item I've ever had against my body and I knew right away that I wanted one like it.

She warned me that they are very expensive but proceeded to tell us where we could get one. The robe reminds me of the one's we see on commercials or movies that show people at places like the Ritz Carlton or the Hilton where they furnish these robes with their emblems on them.

Well, I'll never get to stay at any of those hotels, but I could buy the robe for myself if I tightened up some other areas of my budget. (If I just cut out one medicine for a month, no, I guess that's not the answer.) My daughters always encourage me to indulge myself in some of my whimsies. Sherry sort of hinted that maybe I would get one of the robes for my birthday in October or for Christmas.

The robe had already spoiled me enough that I didn't want to wait. This was only May and there would still be some chilly mornings and evenings when the warmth of this robe would save me having to turn the heat pump or gas logs on.

If I try real hard, I can justify the cost of the robe in what I will save on energy. Fear of being cold has caused me to leave an afghan on the pew at church, a quilt in my car, and I carry a jacket everywhere I go. I have been able to keep my house warm enough, and I thank God for that because I know there are many folks that are not so fortunate.

Mentally I argued with myself all the way to the store in Granite Quarry, but once I tried the robe in the right size and snow white plushy fabric, I was sold. Now the worse thing about this purchase is worrying that I might spill something on it or catch it in the wheelchair. (Some readers may remember my experience when the sweater got caught in the wheels.)

Common sense tells me the robe will not be good to wear while cooking or cleaning. Well, when I'm cold and I put this robe on I'm just thankful that the Lord has enabled me to treat myself to something that gives me such pleasure. I am sad for those who are less fortunate than I am.

THE SCRIPTURE

I attended a church outing and while listening to the devotional, the following scripture caught my attention: In Isaiah 42:16: God says "I will turn the darkness into light before them and make the rough places smooth."

This scripture was referring to the blind; sometimes we are "blind," even when our eyes are "fully functioning." What is "rough" in our lives can be straightened up if we open our eyes to the circumstances, and our hearts to the Lord.

When I ride my scooter on gravel or unpaved surfaces, or at times even paved sidewalks, things get a little bumpy. Time ages roadways just as it does our physical bodies. Spiritual aging, on the other hand, is a "good thing."

Reading scripture over the years has enabled me to "see" (no pun intended) how God works in my life. Publication of my stories and speaking engagements helped me share with others what it is like to have "rough places." Like others who have major health problems, I've learned a lot about having a "rough row to hoe." But I've also learned my purpose in life, and I love telling people how God can make "the rough places smooth."

One friend of mine has experienced twenty years of pain and suffering. When I first met her, she had a lot of anger and doubt. After having her foot amputated, she didn't see how God could use her for anything. She was depressed and struggling with learning to use her prosthesis.

Sometimes if we really "look" we can "see" that there is always someone worse off, either mentally, spiritually, or physically. Helping others will show us how we can be Christ-like and "turn darkness into light."

I believe my friend realized she was a "light" in my life when she made herself available to make cards for the soldiers, to help me run errands, and to share our "heart stories." We talk openly about the "fruits of the spirit," but because I am from the Bible belt of the South, I try to refrain from pushing any particular type of church doctrine down her throat. She says some folks from the South do that and it turns her off.

In the early stages of our friendship, I told her I am a Christian and would talk about my personal relationship with the Lord. I talk…she listens; she talks…I listen. We both share our hopes; the aches, the pains, the good, the bad, and yep, even the "ugly."

I've introduced her to some of my friends who have serious health problems, but their "rough places" are made smoother because of their relationship with the Lord. They have found how God uses them. One of "the other Linda's" in my life is like those "candles that never burn out." She's a great listener and a "sounding board" for my stories, and other issues. I know I am in her prayers and she knows likewise.

I like to tell people that I am not "the brightest light bulb in the box." But I also know that God is, and He certainly can turn the "darkness into light" even in the worse health problems.

I mentioned to one friend at the church outing that I needed to make sure what scripture the devotion leader had used, since I felt a story coming on. He asked about my vivid imagination, and how I knew this would turn into a story from scripture. What can I say: "All scripture is God-breathed, whether we hear His voice or not."

THE SOLITUDE OF COUNTRY LIVING

Everyone wants to know why I have a "For Sale" sign in the yard at my little doll house. I've only had a few calls. Everyone loves the yard and the "curb appeal." One man asked me to please tell him that the house is "bigger" than it looks. I told him I could only say that if he wants me to lie to him, and I'm not a very good liar.

The doll house is just slightly over 1,000 square feet and has only two tiny bedrooms, and one very large handicapped accessible bathroom. It has extra wide doors and hallway, but I've still scarred them with the wheelchairs and scooters. There are raised ceilings except in the bathroom, bedrooms, and closets. This does give the house a larger airier look.

The living and dining rooms are very comfortable, but the kitchen is tiny. I wish I had made the cabinets, bars, etc. more handicapped accessible, but I didn't know when I moved in that I would have a full-fledged multiple sclerosis exacerbation four months later.

There is a nice-sized washer/dryer area and three closets. There is a set of gas logs that can heat the house very comfortably, and the gas pack, heat/water, and air conditioning are fairly inexpensive to operate. If I would get rid of some of my junk, the house would be perfect for me.

I am very proud of my beautiful yard. Some folks have asked who my landscaper was. Well, I can't do all the heavy work, but I did most of the planning for how it is now. The house and yard are as nice as I can afford to make them, although I always love more flowers.

There's just one problem; I'm kind of like a child...I want my cake, but I want to eat it too. I love living in the house and working and relaxing in the yard. But I don't have the transportation or freedom to come and go like I want to. I love the solitude of country living, but when I want to go somewhere, I am stranded unless someone is available to take me where I want or need to go. Living alone has its advantages, but when I first moved here, I was still driving and I want to drive again now

The answer is a disability van and I'm trying to make a decision about whether I want to face that debt every month. Freedom is a precious thing, and it can be expensive in many ways, but my time may or may not be short. I know there are many shut-ins in this world, but I guess I'm just not ready to be one. I know that my speaking engagements and my stories have helped reach people for the Lord, but I can only have so many contacts here in my little doll house.

These handicapped conversion vans are very expensive, but if I make another major change I can start going to church again. My first book is going over very well and this would enable me to travel to support groups to share how God can get them through crisis as He has me.

This is another of those times when one can see God at work. As I was talking with the owner about the purchase of the conversion van, he offered to display my book in his showrooms as he deals with disabled people everyday. (Who would have thought my book would be displayed in the lobby of an automobile dealership?) Well, the sell of the books could help the expense of traveling.

Also, there is the possibility that if I can travel with my books, they may help pay for the van. But the most important thing is that in these last years of my life, I can once again reach those who are lost in their disabilities, and lead them to a personal relationship with our Lord and Savior where they can find peace and acceptance with their pain. As I've said before, putting my stories in a book to sell isn't all about money; it's how God can use me to glorify Him.

If it is God's will, things will work out, and I will enjoy the solitude of country living, but also some restored freedom.

THE SOURCE OF MY FRUSTRATION

I'm sure we've all been frustrated at one time or another about something in our lives, but I think I've found being handicapped has been the biggest cause of frustration in my life today. Since 1993 when my husband died, I became more and more independent, but the major multiple sclerosis attack in 2002 took a lot of that from me.

Back in my twenties when myasthenia gravis caused extreme muscle weakness, I thought one of my biggest losses was the ability to dance, even though I seldom had the opportunity to go dancing. I can remember though how I would dance around in my house as I did my cleaning and listened to music. But then in 2002 when multiple sclerosis took away my ability to walk, dancing seemed to be of no major importance.

Things continued to change (both good and bad), and I've accepted the use of wheelchairs and scooters. Then someone says, "I wish I had one of those," and I just smile and say to myself, "Yeah, and I wish I had your set of good legs." So my loyal friends wonder "Why is she so down now?"

Well, it came about like this. I finally had a new scooter that can be folded up in the trunk of a car, and only the second opportunity of my life to spend a whole week at the beach. It was March and the weather was kind of "iffy," so I got dressed one morning to sit in a lounge chair overlooking the ocean (my favorite place in the whole world).

It warmed up some, so I decided to return to my room, put on my new swimsuit, and go down by the pool. That has been another source of frustration when I poured hot grits on my leg right after wearing the *elegant* swimsuit one time. (My brother, Michael, had picked out the swimsuit, and said "That's an elegant looking swimsuit.") I have to admit I liked the way I looked before the burn.

Now, four months later, the burn was not healed, so I still could not go in the pool, but with a pair of shorts, I could sit in the sun in the swimsuit. (As usual, I ramble on, but back to the first point of frustration.)

I went to the room, put on the swimsuit (which is not an easy thing for a disabled person to do), and got back on my scooter, only to discover the battery was dead. There I was, alone in the room, all dressed to go out to the pool…no working scooter…dead legs, and I couldn't even reach the plug to charge the scooter. Fortunately, I did have a wheelchair close by; and made the transfer, fussing as I did so.

So what did this frustrated old lady do? I called for help. The resort had already helped by rearranging furniture, and God had answered prayer for some spring-like weather. A maintenance man came, plugged in the scooter, and wheeled me down to the pool. The wind there was a little chilly, so he searched and found me a place where I could catch a few rays of sunshine without being directly exposed to the wind.

Regardless of how frustrated one gets, if a handicapped person is willing to ask for help, God will send an angel to replace the frustration with acts of kindness. God continues to bless me with wonderful folks who receive their blessings through service to others.

In spite of my frustration and disability, I continue to be blessed by our Lord and Savior Jesus Christ who helps me master periods of frustration.

THE THORN

Do you, or have you ever, had a "thorn in your flesh." I don't mean a splinter, but a large painful *thorn.* In Second Corinthians 12:1-10, we learn about the Apostle Paul's vision, and the thorn in his flesh. Paul had "revelations from the Lord." Because of these "surpassingly great revelations," he believed the thorn in his flesh was to keep him from becoming conceited, and was a messenger from Satan, there to torment him.

Three times he pleaded with the Lord to take the thorn away. But the Lord said, "My grace is sufficient for you, for my power is made perfect in weakness." Paul then says, "Therefore I will boast all the more gladly about my weaknesses, so that Christ's power may rest on me. That is why, for Christ's sake, I delight in weaknesses, in insults, in hardships, in persecutions, in difficulties. For when I am weak, then I am strong."

I bet you may be thinking something like, "I could have read all that in the Bible." I know that is true, but I hope to share how this affects my life, and perhaps the lives of others as well.

If you have ever read my stories, then you know that I have several *large thorns* in my body: myasthenia gravis, multiple sclerosis, an AVM, and now, osteoporosis. Studying God's Word (the Holy Bible), enables us to experience revelations in our own lives, and helps us understand the *whys* of those *thorns* we have to deal with. Have you questioned the Lord about ***the thorns*** in your life?

Reading scripture over the past 16 years has helped me understand that those *thorns* in my flesh are part of God's plans for my life. His purpose has been for me to share *my thorns* with others. Through the years, He taught me to overcome most of my fears; led a shy young girl to speak in public to tell people about Him, and to empathize with those who need encouragement. Learning to accept pain and our limitations is an ongoing process. If things get better, our attitude improves. Then we face another valley, and the going gets rough again. At times, anger and bitterness consume us and our *thorns* pierce us even deeper. So what can we do?

It helps if we have a *prayer warrior* that can intervene and help us face each step we have to take to reach our destination. I have several friends who keep me in their prayers. While writing this story, I was reminded how "the other Linda" in my life is a great listener to the first drafts of my stories. She helps me think of more things that need to be added for my stories to meet their destination. What is your final destination? Well, mine is an eternal home in heaven. I wish I could say that "I delight in weaknesses, in insults, in hardships, in persecutions, in difficulties." Reading God's Word and listening to the testimonies of other Christians has enabled me to accept these *thorns,* whether I delight in them or not. I remind myself that others suffer even more than I do.

And God gives us the grace to endure the tests that we are confronted with because of the *thorns* in our flesh. My friend, Linda, says she was once told in a Bible study that sometimes it is people in our lives who are the *thorns* in our flesh. I guess there could be some truth in that as I'm sure most of us have had some *thorny* issues with people in whom we have contact.

She and I agreed, however, that without the tests we suffer through, there would be no testimony for us to share with others. My *thorns* have definitely been my testimony, and I pray that God will continue to use me to help others find the peace He has given me, even when my pain is at its worse.

THE THREE R'S:
REST, RELAX AND REMEMBER

When my oldest daughter was putting my old stories on the computer for the book, she asked why I hadn't written any stories about the many trips made to Stone Mountain, North Carolina. I told her she needed to write her own memories, but she seemed disappointed that I had not.

As a family of four, we took a lot of day trips or weekend getaways to out-of-the way places. My husband and I were never big fans of expensive tourist traps, though we visited a few over the years

Stone Mountain was just a short distance away, and required only a little gas to get there. We could take a picnic and spend the day playing in the water and woods. Joe and the girls loved to slide down the rocks into the cold mountain water. Not me! Back then, I was terrified of water and I always got cold in the mountains. I was willing to go along though, because they all loved the place so much.

Sherry and I remember three particular incidents that took place. She still carries a scar on her leg from the time her dad was chasing her through the woods. She took a pretty bad fall and that spoiled an otherwise perfect day. We were fortunate that it did not require stitches.

Then there was the weekend that we took our pop-up camper, planning to spend a couple of nights. Our sharpest memory is sitting in that camper with a terrible storm raging all around. The mountain creeks were rising and the tent cover was leaking. We were trying to play board games to keep the girls from getting bored, and so we would not dwell on the thunder, lightning, and rising water. Before the storm was over, we had to pack up a wet camper and leave soaking wet. I was relieved to arrive home safely, but there was no pleasure in unpacking the wet canvas and other equipment in the bright sunshine.

Those incidents were nothing compared to the misfortune of some other folks. Some young guys were diving and one took a serious fall. An ambulance took forever arriving and we watched the young fellow being carried out on a stretcher. We had no way of finding out what the end results were for him, but we knew the hospital was quite some distance away.

I told Sherry most of our memories are different. She only remembers the fun, but I also remember the work associated with packing and unpacking. Even the day trips required preparation of food, dry clothes, towels, etc.

Sherry doesn't remember how much the myasthenia gravis limited my physical activities. When they hiked or played in the water, I sat waiting, pretending not to mind being left alone.

THE *WHAT IFS* AND *MAYBES*

I wrote about the "I Cans" and "I Can'ts" so it came to my mind to write about the *What Ifs* and *Maybes*. This is kind of like daydreaming except as a child this was more like an evening fantasy just before sleep took over.

I used to lie awake wondering "what if" this or that or something else. Since I lived in a dysfunctional home, the "what ifs" were always good things that took me where I thought I wanted to go. Looking back, some of those "what ifs" were Cinderella dreams.

I don't usually write fiction, but I guess "what ifs" are somewhat fictitious so these pipe dreams start back from my beginning as follows:

"What if" my real father and my mother had married? "Maybe" my whole life would have been different. Since I never knew him, I don't know if it would have been better or worse, but God knows.

"What if" my mother had allowed my aunt to adopt me? There is no "maybe."

My life would have been totally different. I would have grown up in Greensboro and would never have been dragging town that cruising day when I met my husband.

"What if" there had been no Joe in my life; then there would have been no Sherry, Sonya, Billy, Hobie, or Hallie Renee, my new granddaughter.

"What if" I had joined the Air Force as I had planned to do before Joe and I met? "Maybe" my health problems would have caused me to be discharged.

"What if" I had gone to college; "maybe" I would have been a librarian, reporter, or teacher. "Maybe" I would have made a difference in the lives of children as my daughter, the teacher, is doing.

"What if" I had never been a wife, mother, or grandmother; I would have suffered the greatest losses of my life.

"What if" I had never had Myasthenia Gravis, surgery or a staff infection? "Maybe" I would never have suffered the physical or emotional strife that I underwent, or that which I put my family through.

"What if" Joe had not died with cancer at age forty-seven? "Maybe" we would have suffered through the last 16 years of health problems and traveled together down the road of raising our grandchildren. Despite the bad times, "maybe" we would have continued to have good times because our love was so strong. We were bonded together through so many hard times.

"What if" I had never had to go on disability and had worked all these years since 1979? What would I have gained, or lost?

"What if" Joe and I had got to take our other dream trips to Alaska and Hawaii? (Well, I did go to Hawaii without Joe, but I'm glad I went when I could still travel.)

"What if" I had not had seizures and multiple sclerosis? I would not have stories to tell or a life history to speak about. What would I do with my time? How would it feel to be normal?

"What if" I had met someone and remarried? Who knows where that might have taken me? I don't want to know. I have too many reasons not to go there.

"What if" there is never romance in my life again? That's okay; been there, done that with the love of my life.

I could go on and on, but "maybe" my audience might already be bored. Thoughts like these can be a pleasant interlude as long as we can let go at the right time.

I have been successful in putting the "what ifs" of the past behind me, and I just live day by day. Who knows, when I'm in the mood again, I might think and write about the "what ifs" in my future. Stay tuned.

THE YEAR IS OVER

One year ends and another one begins and time marches on. The newspaper business is changing and there is less space for writers like me who are not paid reporters. My stories, at this point, are still in *PrimeTime*, *Senior Savy*, and the *Cleveland Chronicle*.

First, where did the year go? Time seems to pass so much quicker now than it once did. When we were young, it seemed like the school week and then the work week both went at a snail's pace.

Riding the Rowan Transportation Van on Tuesday's and Friday's to run errands takes a chunk out of my week, but gives me a lot to write about. I'm usually so tired when I get home that my body begs for a nap.

There are those mornings when I wake up between 6:00 and 8:00 a.m. Usually, I do my devotions, eat breakfast, and later take a morning nap. When folks call before 10:00 a.m., they ask why I'm still asleep. They can't believe I've already put a load of clothes in the washer, unloaded and loaded the dishwasher, and some days have even swept and mopped my floors before I went back to sleep.

If I do need to type a story, early morning is the best time for me to sit at the computer before my pain becomes too noticeable. I still write with pen and paper in my recliner before I record my stories on the computer. (My fingers still type a little faster than my brain puts my thoughts together.) Over the years, some folks have thought I got paid for my stories but I have only had a few that I sold to magazines.

Well, a few interesting things have been happening. Watching others open their gifts was a special time for me. I finally found the 4-H Precious Moments doll that my two daughters have been wanting for many years. During their childhood, 4-H was such a special part of our lives as a family.

Santa Claus was really good to me this year. I received several nice surprises and even bought myself a thing or two. It was an interesting chain of events that went like this: A reader of one of my stories called and wanted to give me something that I could use when potting my plants. She had read that I was using an old plastic chair and she had a *real* potting station that she had hardly used and needed to get out of her garage. I think it will be perfect for me

As soon as I saw her face, I knew we had gone to high school together over forty years ago. We had not realized we knew each other because of our married names, but it was nice sharing some memories. This was such a thoughtful deed. I offered to pay Diane and she could probably have sold it at a yard sale, but she wanted to give it to me because she has enjoyed my stories. One thing is for sure, when we were in high school together, I never thought I would be a writer or that folks would do such nice things for me.

On the way home from picking up this gift, we stopped at a little country store that was having a yard sale. I used to love going to yard sales, but seldom do since my husband passed away because it is so hard for me to get around. But for some reason, I asked my daughter to stop at this one. The first thing I spotted was a metal bench with an arbor over it. I just knew it would be too expensive, but it was reduced to half-price for the holidays, so I decided to treat myself. I had to find someone with a truck to deliver it, and my sister and her family took care of that. (They are all so good to me and do so much to help me.)

We went back through town to treat ourselves to some ice cream, and I spotted a sidewalk greenhouse at the Okie-Dokie Shop. I mentioned to my daughter that I might buy myself one of those someday. A couple days before Christmas, Santa came early, and left the greenhouse in my driveway. (She had been asking what I would like to have for Christmas, but I would never have asked her to buy me something that expensive.)

On Christmas Eve at our family gathering, my other daughter and her family gave me some great supplies for my card ministry. Sonya was the one who first heard about this project on the radio, and encouraged me to check into sending cards to our soldiers in Iraq. (I've received many thank you notes from the soldiers and I know now I'm doing God's will.)

Another month is about over and I'm just finishing this story. Blessings continue to fall upon me. I've already received requests to speak at various places. These requests are results of my stories, and I continue to be amazed at how the Lord has used my life experiences to reach out to others. I know if it is God's will, I will be able to work out travel and other problems; and another month will be here and gone before I know it.

Once again, I continue to give thanks to the reason for the season, our Lord and Savior Jesus Christ.

THE HEALING TOUCH

I've never had a desire to be a nurse, doctor, or anything else, in the medical field. I've had a few friends through the years that said I should have been a counselor. Doctors and nurses all over the state of North Carolina have taken care of me during numerous health problems, and I admire their dedication and devotion to their patients.

There are times when sick people, and even their caregivers, need to remember that God is the Great Physician of all times and, contrary to the doctors in today's world, He still makes house calls. God helped these physicians and nurses make the necessary choices to acquire their education, and helped them find their employment. Just as God had plans for these folks, He also has *business plans* for others, like me.

Once again, on a low day spiritually, I heard my favorite preacher discuss "Living Life as a Healer." Immediately, God got my attention and I saw myself in this sermon.

Once upon a time, I was a secretary, but when I became physically unable to work professionally, I became a volunteer. I didn't realize at that time, but God knew He was providing my *education* during those years when I was a volunteer 4-H leader. Standing up as a leader in front of a bunch of children was my *public education.*

When my daughters picked Public Speaking as their main project area, I never suspected that someday the Lord would call me to practice in the business of "The Great Commission." (Matthew 28:18-20) He removed the *butterflies* from my stomach and I traveled for six years talking to women about The Plan of Salvation, and helped many to make a commitment to the Lord.

And then along came my college education in the *School of Hard Knocks.* The past seven years of physical pain, depression, fear and anxiety have enabled me to emphasize with those who need *healing.*

This sermon seemed to be speaking directly to my heart and I remembered a pastor putting himself in a conversation with God. I listened as the preacher gave me further education in talking (or better yet, listening) to God's instruction.

"Linda, God can use you as a *healer*. You can take *healing* wherever you go; you are a *healer!* Go ahead; smile and talk to strangers; initiate a conversation. Linda, you can exhibit healing in your hands and voice. You can pray for others; you can help them wipe away their tears and depression."

By the time this sermon was over, I knew that I do have a *divine appointment.* I can put myself *in the shoes* of other troubled or handicapped people. I can *encourage the discouraged* by listening with my heart. Knowing that I have helped in the emotional healing of some readers, I have been encouraged to travel with my book to speak with support groups. I realize the possibility of more health problems when traveling, and I know there are some risk factors. But I refuse to live in fear. I believe that God has plans for me to get "back into the world" to share with others His power to heal.

I'm sure there are probably some scoffers who think I give myself too much credit, but it is God himself who has given me the events to write about, and the opportunities to share His word. Now I just have to trust Him to make the arrangements necessary for me to travel.

You may or may not have noticed that this story is out of alphabetical order; that is because God provided this lesson right before the book was sent for publication. To God be the glory!

www.ingramcontent.com/pod-product-compliance
Lightning Source LLC
LaVergne TN
LVHW091006080826
845145LV00003B/1147

* 9 7 8 0 5 7 8 0 3 4 5 7 7 *